MW01139393

PUMAS
ON THE HUNT

by Jody Sullivan Rake

Reading Consultant:
Barbara J. Fox
Reading Specialist
North Carolina State University

Content Consultant:
Sara L. Carlson
Director of Programs & Operations
The Cougar Fund
Jackson, Wyoming

CAPSTONE PRESS
a capstone imprint

Blazers is published by Capstone Press,
151 Good Counsel Drive, P.O. Box 669, Mankato, Minnesota 56002.
www.capstonepress.com

092009
005619WZS10

Library of Congress Cataloging-in-Publication Data
Rake, Jody Sullivan.
    Pumas : on the hunt / by Jody Sullivan Rake.
    p. cm. — (Blazers. Killer animals)
    Summary: "Describes pumas, their habitat, hunting habits, and relationship
to people" — Provided by publisher.
    Includes bibliographical references and index.
    ISBN 978-1-4296-3928-6 (library binding)
    1. Puma — Juvenile literature. I. Title.
QL737.C23R35 2010
599.75'24 — dc22   2009027861

Editorial Credits
Mandy Robbins, editor; Kyle Grenz, designer; Svetlana Zhurkin, media researcher;
    Laura Manthe, production specialist

Photo Credits
Alamy/Papilio, 8, 18–19
Corbis/Charles Krebs, 22–23; Chase Swift, 4–5; Terry W. Eggers, cover
Peter Arnold/Biosphoto/J.-L. Klein & M.-L. Hubert, 14–15
Photolibrary/Peter Bisset, 20–21; Thomas Kitchin & Victoria Hurst, 6–7, 24–25
Shutterstock/Dennis Donohue, 12–13, 26–27; Joy Fera, 17; Melanie DeFazio, 28–29;
    Ronnie Howard, 10–11

TABLE OF CONTENTS

MANY NAMES, ONE COOL CAT

Just before dawn, a deer grazes
in a cool, grassy meadow. Nearby,
a puma watches closely.

KILLER FACT

Pumas are also called cougars, panthers, and mountain lions.

In one leap, the puma is on top of the deer. The deer tries to run, but the puma has it by the throat. One minute later, the hunt is over.

MIGHTY MEAT-EATERS

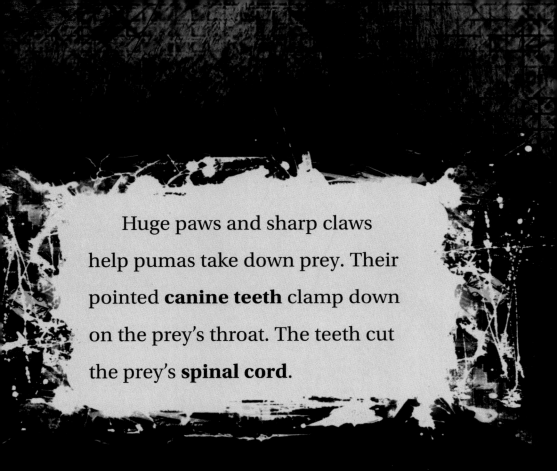

Huge paws and sharp claws help pumas take down prey. Their pointed **canine teeth** clamp down on the prey's throat. The teeth cut the prey's **spinal cord**.

canine teeth – sharp teeth used to tear meat

spinal cord – a thick cord of nerves that carries signals between the brain and other nerves in the body

Pumas are the largest cats in North and South America. They stand 2 feet (.6 meter) tall at the shoulder.

Females weigh about 100 pounds (45 kilograms). Males reach about 150 pounds (68 kilograms).

KILLER FACT

Pumas are amazing jumpers. A puma can leap 18 feet (5.5 meters) straight up into a tree.

Pumas have quick bodies
and strong legs. These features
make them mighty runners and
jumpers. Pumas can run up to
45 miles (72 kilometers) per hour.

Puma Diagram

thick fur

sharp claws

14

HUNTING BY LEAPS AND BOUNDS

Pumas usually hunt between sunset and dawn. Their amazing eyesight helps them search for prey. Even in the dark, a puma's sight is its strongest sense.

KILLER FACT

Puma eyes have a reflecting layer of cells.
These cells double the amount of light
the eyes receive.

Pumas **stalk** their prey. The puma quietly watches and waits. Then it pounces on the prey's back and kills it quickly.

stalk – to hunt an animal in a quiet, secret way

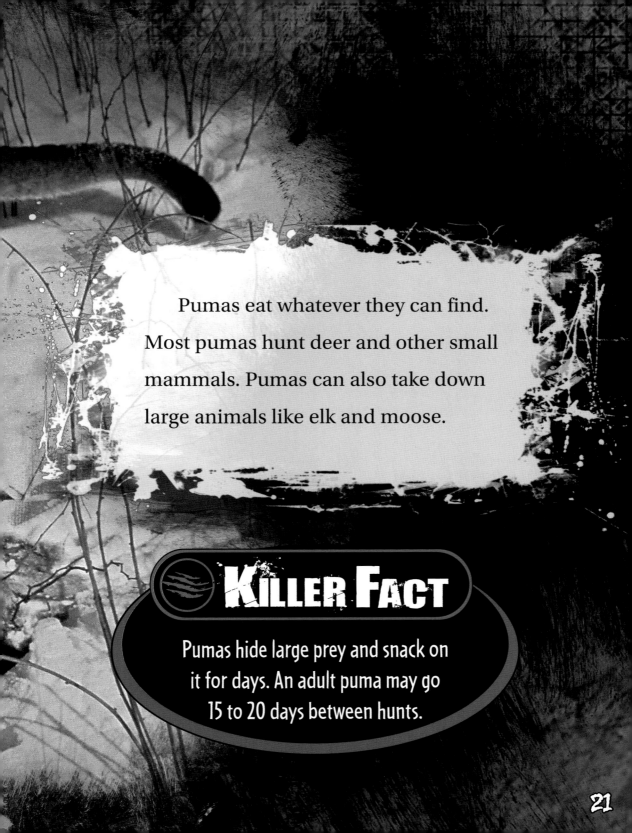

Pumas eat whatever they can find. Most pumas hunt deer and other small mammals. Pumas can also take down large animals like elk and moose.

KILLER FACT

Pumas hide large prey and snack on it for days. An adult puma may go 15 to 20 days between hunts.

PUMAS IN DANGER

Pumas play an important part in the **ecosystem**. In places where humans don't hunt, pumas help control the number of deer. Otherwise, many deer would starve or die of disease.

ecosystem – a group of animals and plants that work together with their surroundings

23

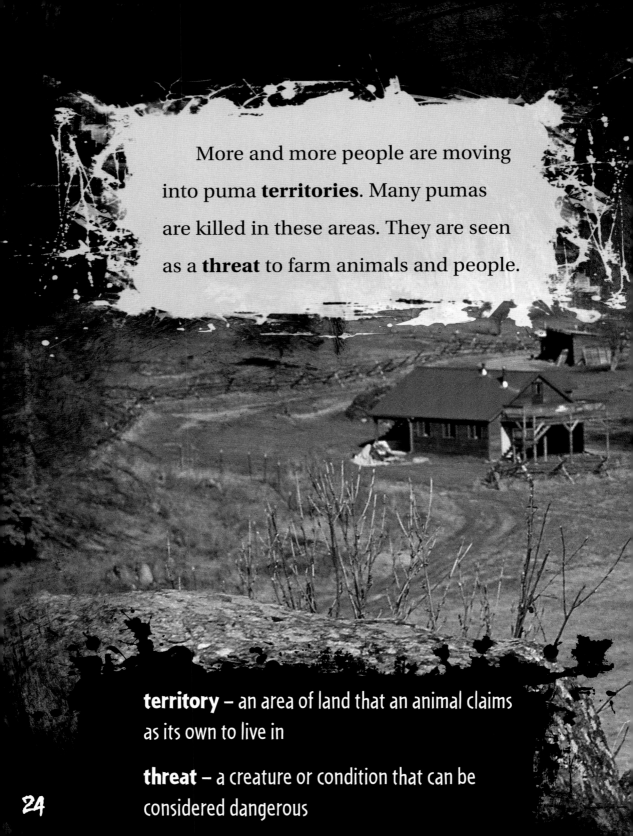

More and more people are moving into puma **territories**. Many pumas are killed in these areas. They are seen as a **threat** to farm animals and people.

territory – an area of land that an animal claims as its own to live in

threat – a creature or condition that can be considered dangerous

KILLER FACT

The Florida panther is the only puma found in the eastern United States. Only about 100 of these animals are alive today.

Pumas try to avoid people. People who respect these powerful **predators** can help pumas survive in the future.

predator – an animal that hunts and eats other animals

KILLER FACT

Pumas purr and hiss just like pet cats do.

Ready to Pounce!

GLOSSARY

canine teeth (KAY-nyn TEETH) — sharp teeth used to tear meat

ecosystem (EE-koh-sis-tuhm) — a group of animals and plants that work together with their surroundings

predator (PRED-uh-tur) — an animal that hunts and eats other animals

prey (PRAY) — an animal that is hunted by another animal as food

spinal cord (SPINE-uhl KORD) — a thick cord of nerves that carries signals between the brain and other nerves in the body

stalk (STAWK) — to hunt an animal in a quiet, secret way

territory (TER-uh-tor-ee) — an area of land that an animal claims as its own to live in

threat (THRET) — a creature or condition that can be considered to be dangerous

READ MORE

Macken, JoAnn Early. *Cougars.* Animals that Live in the Mountains. Pleasantville, N.Y.: Gareth Stevens, 2009.

Markle, Sandra. *Mountain Lions.* Animal Predators. Minneapolis: Lerner, 2009.

Rodriguez, Cindy. *Cougars.* Eye to Eye with Endangered Species. Vero Beach, Fla.: Rourke, 2009.

INTERNET SITES

FactHound offers a safe, fun way to find Internet sites related to this book. All of the sites on FactHound have been researched by our staff.

Here's all you do:

Visit *www.facthound.com*

FactHound will fetch the best sites for you!

INDEX